BRANCH LINES AROUND GOSPORT

GOSPORT

Vic Mitchell and Keith Smith

Published in 1986 to celebrate the tenth anniversary of the foundation of the Gosport Railway Society.

Cover design – Deborah Goodridge

First published October 1986

ISBN 0 906520 36 3

© Middleton Press, 1986

Typeset by CitySet - Bosham 573270

Published by Middleton Press
        Easebourne Lane
        Midhurst, West Sussex
        GU29 9AZ
        073 081 3169

Printed & bound by Biddles Ltd,
        Guildford and Kings Lynn

CONTENTS

ACKNOWLEDGEMENTS

Our grateful thanks go to the photographers and collectors mentioned in captions for the help received. These include officers of the Gosport Railway Society and staff of the Gosport Museum. As always, we thank Mrs. E. Fisk, R. Randell, N. Stanyon and our wives for assistance in production. Tickets are reproduced with the kind co-operation of:

G. Croughton

C. R. Gordon-Stuart

N. Langridge

GEOGRAPHICAL SETTING

Gosport is situated at the end of a peninsula, which is the western one of four similar projections, the other being Selsey Bill, Hayling Island and Portsea. With a maximum altitude of under 50ft., the terrain presented no great problems to the railway engineers. This album is the last to cover the railways of these "peninsulas" and offers an opportunity to see that, although similar geographical features prevailed, it was the suitability of Portsmouth Harbour for Naval purposes that caused its shores to be developed to the greater extent.

The population of the Gosport area in 1840 was about 13,000 and by 1950 had reached 58,000. This railway-less town now has around 80,000 inhabitants, about three times that of the county town of West Sussex and one third of that of Portsmouth.

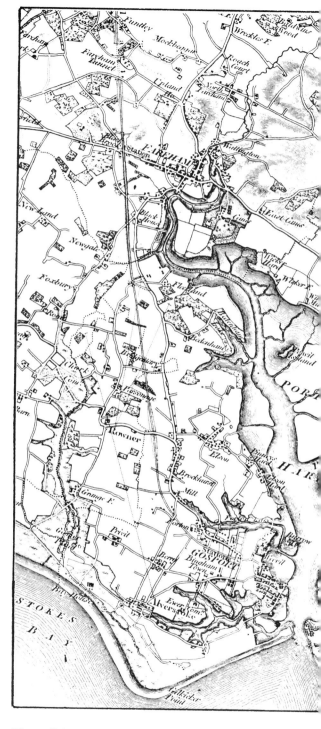

First edition Ordnance Survey with the 1841 railway superimposed on it. 1" to 1 mile.

HISTORICAL BACKGROUND

Branch Line to Gosport

This was the first railway in the Portsmouth area and was a branch from the London & South Western Railway's route from London to Southampton. It left the main line at Bishopstoke (later to be renamed Eastleigh) and was opened on 29th November 1841, only to be closed again four days later, due to the collapse of a tunnel north of Fareham, which is described in our *Branch Lines to Alton*. It was reopened on 7th February 1842 and formed Portsmouth's link with London. The branch ceased to be of such importance for passenger traffic when the line from Fareham to Portsmouth via Cosham was opened in 1848. However it continued to play a vital role in carrying varied freight to the Naval victualling and armament yards at Gosport.

Passenger services dwindled until withdrawn on 8th June 1953, the last train running on the 6th. Freight continued to be taken to Gosport until 6th January 1969; thereafter trains ran as far as the Bedenham Naval branch only.

Stokes Bay Branch

The Stokes Bay Railway & Pier Co. was formed in 1855 to allow trains to run direct to an Isle of Wight ferry terminal. (Portsmouth Harbour station did not open until 1876.) Various delays prevented the opening until 6th April 1863 and arrangements were made for the LSWR to operate the service. Initially all trains ran into Gosport and were reversed, but eventually a triangular junction was completed so that trains could run direct onto the branch. Gosport residents, annoyed at their reduction in service, demanded a station be opened at the north end of the branch.

The LSWR took a 999 year lease of the line in 1871 and purchased it in 1875. The scheme was never a financial success, remaining a secondary route until closed on 30th October 1915.

Lee-on-the-Solent Railway

Powers were obtained in 1890, under the Railway Construction Facilities Act of 1864, to build a three mile single line branch from Fort Brockhurst to the embryonic coastal resort. It was opened on 12th May 1894 by the Lee-on-the-Solent Light Railway Company. It was one of the few lines to be built under this Act – another local example being the Selsey Tramway.

The company took the unusual course of buying coaches but hiring locomotives. From 1909, the LSWR leased it and provided all rolling stock until the company was absorbed by the Southern Railway in 1923.

The SR soon applied for powers to close the line but it was not until 1st January 1931 that passenger services ceased, goods facilities at Lee being withdrawn on 28th September 1935.

←

1. This well known engraving of the railway terminus and hotel is worth repeating as it shows the south elevation with its original arrangement of arches. (Gosport Railway Society coll.)

PASSENGER SERVICES

The early service on the London to Southampton route was eight trains a day, most of which had Gosport connections.

By 1863, there were five trains on the branch on weekdays with two on Sundays. All reversed at Gosport to serve Stokes Bay, although the Sunday service was withdrawn on 1st August.

By 1896, the branch had eleven trains each way, Stokes Bay having four direct and three via Gosport. In 1910, the figures were 14, 2 and 7 respectively.

For some time the LSWR timetable included a named train from Waterloo – "The Exeter, Blandford, Weymouth & Stokes Bay Express" – which divided at Basingstoke and Bishopstoke. In 1913, there were also through coaches from the Midlands.

Gosport was handling 18 trains in 1924 and, by 1938, there were 20 with two additional journeys up to Fort Brockhurst. Destinations included Eastleigh, Romsey and Alton (Waterloo until electrification to Alton).

By the middle of World War II, there were only seven trains and in the final years there were five, two of which operated to Alton. Sunday services had ceased long previously.

Lee-on-the-Solent

A shuttle service to Fort Brockhurst was operated on this branch with stops at the halts being by request. A weekday service of eight return journeys was operated for most of the life of the line, increasing to ten prior to World War I, when a summer Sunday timetable of two or three trains was run.

The 1935 map, at 1 inch to 1 mile scale, shows the Lee-on-the-Solent branch to have been lifted between the pier and the point where it turned inland, at Elmore Halt. The road junction at Privett was the location of Fort Gomer Halt and is now the site of a roundabout. Stokes Bay Pier is shown, but the line between it and Gosport Road station is not.

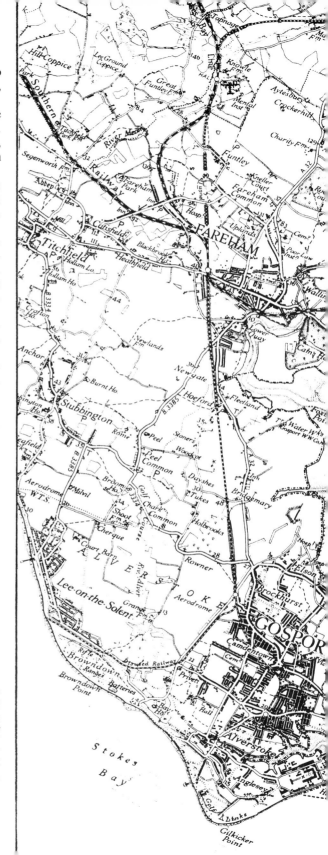

FAREHAM

Fareham Railway Station 22nd March 1861

2. Some artistic licence may have been taken in this engraving as the Railway Hotel, on the right, was three storied and the lower windows of the station have not been seen in living memory. (D. Tillman collection)

The 1910 edition shows on the left (from to to bottom) the 1841 line to Eastleigh via the Knowle Tunnel; the 1904 tunnel avoiding line and the 1889 single line to Netley and Southampton, which was doubled in 1911. On the right, the 1848 route curves west to Portsmouth, the straight tracks being the direct line to Gosport.

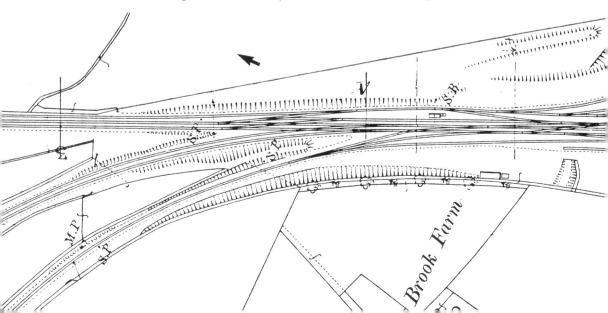

3. There are few photographs of Fareham's shunting horse. This flexible form of motive power had declined in numbers by World War II, when there was a shortage of handlers and trainers. The location of East Box is marked SB, above Brooks Farm. (D. Tillman collection)

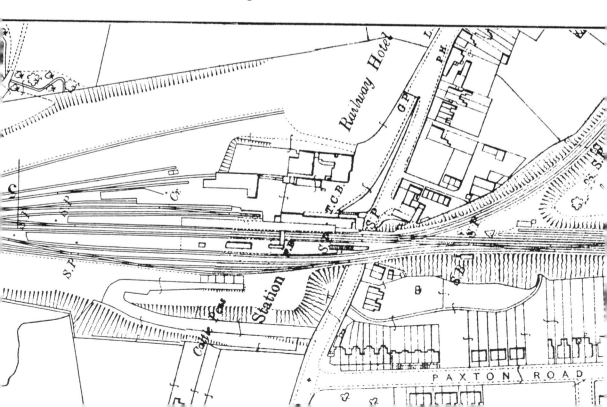

4. A 1928 view from the footbridge shows the straight alignment of the original route to Gosport and also the gates on the island plat- form that were at the top of a flight of steps from the street. (Late E. Wallis)

5. A typical scene from the mid-1930s shows 0–4–2 class A12 no. 623 on a stopping train from Gosport to Alton. The station is still gas lit. (S. C. Nash collection)

6. A photograph from July 1947 reveals the common motive power of the period – class T9. This is no. 726, one of the 4–4–0s nicknamed *Greyhounds*. Other period features shown include the cattle pens and the profusion of porcelain insulators for the exposed copper telephone wires.
(J.H. Aston)

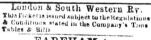

London & South Western Ry.
This Ticket is issued subject to the Regulations & Conditions stated in the Company's Time Tables & Bills
FAREHAM to
LEE ON THE SOLENT
Via Fort Brockhurst
Fareham   Fareham
Lee-on-Solent   Lee-on-Solent
3rd CLASS   (S.2)   3rd CLASS
Fare 6d   Fare 6d

2nd. HALF DAY EXCURSION   HALF DAY EXCURSION 2nd
Ryde Pier
TO
FAREHAM   **RYDE PIER**
Via Portsmouth Har   Via Portsmouth Har
Including Pier Tolls   Including Pier Tolls
Exclusive of   Exclusive of
Tramway or Train   Tramway or Train
(S)   (S)
For conditions see over   For conditions see over

7. A class L12 simmers in the loop as it awaits departure with the 6.12pm to Gosport on 10th April 1948. These small-chimneyed machines were known as *Bulldogs* and were more than adequate for the short trains on the branch. (J.H. Aston)

8. A bay platform was provided on the down side and was used by those Meon Valley services terminating at Fareham. This route was closed to passengers on 5th February 1955, this photograph being taken shortly afterwards. (D. Cullum)

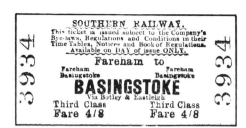

9. Former LBSCR class K 2–6–0 no. 32351 hauls the 10.03 Eastleigh to Fratton freight towards the frost-covered barrow crossing, on 7th January 1961. The local items of interest are the up main starting signals and the steam crane. (D. Fereday Glenn)

10. On 30th April 1961, members of the LCGB enjoyed a railtour from Waterloo via Portsmouth, Gosport, Winchester (Chesil), Newbury and Ascot – all for 52/– (£2.60). Class E1 no. 2694 and class 02 no. 30200 provided the power locally. (A.E. Bennett)

11. An ageing class 700, bearing the letters NBG above its number, hauls the 10.10 am freight to Gosport on 26th July 1961, whilst the signalman from West Box offers up the single line tablet. (D. Fereday Glenn)

12. An unusual and occasional traffic to Gosport was racing pigeons. Here we see a grimy class U 2–6–0 running onto the branch with assorted vans from northern clubs. Station staff were responsible for releasing the birds and recording their departure time. (D. Fereday Glenn)

2nd - PRIVILEGE
SINGLE
PRIVILEGE - 2nd
SINGLE

Fareham to

Fareham
Eastleigh

Fareham
Eastleigh

EASTLEIGH
via Botley

(S)   10d. Fare 10d.   (S)
For conditions see over For conditions see over

1441   1441

British Transport Commission (S)

FAREHAM
PLATFORM TICKET 2d.
Available one hour on day of issue only.
Not valid in trains. Not transferable.
To be given up when leaving platform
For conditions see over

8803   8803

13. The footbridge provided a good vantage point in May 1966 to view the junction and storage sidings beyond. By that time, steps were no longer provided between the two parts of bridge no. 28 but the original station building survived and is still in use today. (D. Cullum)

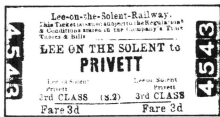

Lee-on-the-Solent-Railway.
This Ticket is issued subject to the Regulations & Conditions stated in the Company's Time Tables & Bills

LEE ON THE SOLENT to
PRIVETT

Lee on Solent Privett	Lee on Solent Privett
3rd CLASS (S.2)	3rd CLASS
Fare 3d	Fare 3d

4543

L108
SOUTHERN RAILWAY.
Commercial Traveller
Available on Day of Issue only

Romsey
to FAREHAM
VIA
Third Class.

0488
SOUTHERN RAILWAY.
Rail Motor Car
This Ticket is issued subject to the Bye-laws, Regulations and Conditions stated in the Company's Time Tables, Bills and Notices.
Available on day of issue only:
THIRD CLASS SINGLE
Fare 2d
BETWEEN
Browndown Halt
and
Lee-on-the-Solent
Fort Gomer Halt
and
Fort Brockhurst
This Ticket must be punched in the section to which the Passenger is entitled to travel and must be shown on demand.

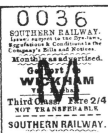

0036
SOUTHERN RAILWAY.
Issue subject to the Bye-laws, Regulations & Conditions in the Company's Bills and Notices.
Monthly as advertised.
Gosport to
WICKHAM
Via Fareham
Third Class. Fare 2/4
NOT TRANSFERABLE
SOUTHERN RAILWAY.
MONTHLY RETURN.
Wickham Gosport
Wickham to
GOSPORT
Via Fareham
Third Class. Fare 2/4
0036

14. The lattice posts and unequal brackets are worthy of closer examination. The white diamond indicated the provision of track circuiting and thus the fireman of a delayed locomotive was not required to remind the signalman of its position. (D. Cullum)

→

16. Signalman Ron Corben gives the bell code to the next box, in July 1969. The chain above his head was pulled to switch on the gas light. The box ceased to function on 5th December 1971 and was eventually demolished. (J.H. Bird)

15. The West Box controlled entry to the branch and was a block post on the main line. Although geographically to the east of the signal box at the north of the station, it was so named by the LSWR because Waterloo was at the *east* of their system and boxes nearest to London were all designated *East*.
(J. Scrace)

→

17. A view from the signal box window cleaning platform, in September 1969, shows no. D6579 returning from Gosport with the daily freight. The sidings on the left had been disused for over a year by then. (J.H. Bird)

18. A few moments laters, the driver surrenders the single line token for the branch. When the signal box was closed, a ground frame was provided, a few yards to the north. (J.H. Bird)

20. No. 47335 starts its journey down the remains of the branch on 9th May 1980. Only the up line had been in use since the singling in 1934, but part of the down track on the right was retained as a siding. The points at the bottom of the picture were part of a crossover which formed a run-round loop. (J. Scrace)

19. Another turn of the film shows the same train entering the station and also the revised track layout following the installation of new steel bridge spans on 10th March 1968. This increased the radius of the curve on the up main line, as all westbound trains then used the former loop platform. (J.H. Bird)

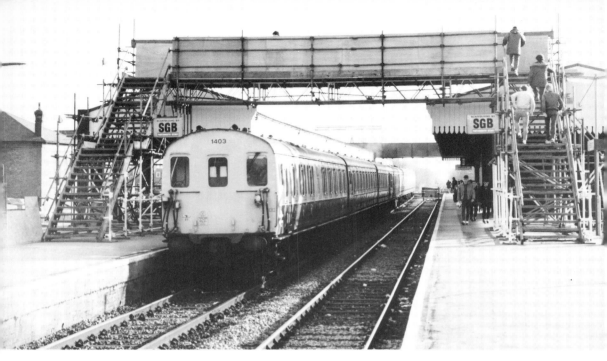

21. During the winter of 1983-84, a temporary footbridge was erected so that major repairs could be carried out on the earlier structure. Two 3-car DEMUs stand in the down platform, bound for Portsmouth. (D.J. Kemp)

23. A railtour by the Southern Electric Group in December 1985 had a seasonable if corny name of the "Ewell Log". No. 33016 hauls it over the up span of bridge no. 28 and passes the branch shunt signal. The former up main platform is now used for terminating a few trains from Eastleigh – the buffer stops are visible in the foreground. (D.J. Kemp)

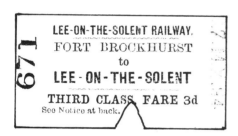

LEE-ON-THE-SOLENT RAILWAY.
FORT BROCKHURST
to
LEE - ON - THE - SOLENT
THIRD CLASS FARE 3d
See Notice at back.
671

22. No. 50043 *Eagle* was a rare sight at Fareham on 24th May 1984. It was hauling a Ledbury to Portsmouth excursion and is seen passing the stone terminal that was opened in the former goods yard. The yard once had a gantry crane capable of lifting 10 tons. (D.J. Kemp)

SOUTHERN RAILWAY.
This Ticket is issued subject to the By-laws Regulations & Conditions stated in the Company's Time Tables Bills & Notices
Available on DAY of issue ONLY.
GOSPORT to
Gosport
Lee on Solent
LEE ON THE SOLENT
Via Fort Brockhurst
Third Class   Third Class
Fare 7d   Fare 7d
0066   9900

24. A Gosport bound freight is seen on Redlands Lane bridge, hauled by Q class no. 30543. The limit of the berthing siding formed from the former down line is evident. (D. Fereday Glenn)

25. A small arch was provided over Newgate Lane, ¾ mile south of Fareham. The train is a SCTS rail tour on 20th February 1966 and is seen returning from Gosport behind N class 2–6–0 no. 31411. (J. Scrace)

26. Freight services had shrunk by the time we see no. 33115 passing behind the houses of Bridgemary, two miles from Fareham, on 16th April 1984. The view is south west from the Gregson arch. (D.J. Kemp)

FAREHAM and GOSPORT.—Southern.

Week Days only.

Miles		mrn	mrn	mrn	mrn	mrn	mrn	mrn	aft	mrn		aft	aft	aft	aft	aft	aft	aft	aft	aft	aft	
	170London(W.)173dep.	....	4 50	5 40	5 50	7 0	8 30	9 10	....	9 30		1145	1 30	2 0	3 30	4 20	5 30	....	....	6 34	7 s 30	...
—	Fareham..........dep.	7 40	8 15	8 33	9 33	1020	1110	1142	1225	1247	1 22	...	2 33	3 52	5 10	6 0	6 45	7 45	....	8 50	9 26	10s31
3¼	Fort Brockhurst166....	7 47	8 22	8 45	9 45	1027	1117	1149	1232	1254	1 29	1 43	2 40	3 59	5 17	6 7	6 52	7 52	8 59	8 57	9 33	10s38
4¼	Gosport ....arr.	7 51	8 26	8 49	9 49	1031	1121	1153	1236	1258	1 33	1 46	2 44	4 3	5 21	6 11	6 56	7 56	8 22	9 1	9 37	10s42

Week Days only.

Miles		mrn	mrn	mrn	mrn	mrn	mrn	mrn	mrn	aft	aft	aft	aft	aft	aft	aft	aft	aft	aft	aft	
—	Gosport...........dep.	6 20	7 35	8 55	9 0	9 23	9 55	1045	1140	1215	1 7	1 30	2 20	2 30	4 0	4 40	5 35	7 15	7 45	8 10	9s30	...
½	Fort Brockhurst...[174	6 24	7 39	8 4	8 59	9 3	9 29	9 59	1049	1144	1219	1 11	1 34	2 23	2 34	4 4	4 44	5 39	7 19	7 44	8 14	9s34
4¼	Fareham 170, 173, arr.	6 31	7 46	8 11	9 6	...	9 36	10 6	1056	1151	1226	1 18	1 41	....	2 41	4 11	4 51	5 46	7 26	7 51	8 24	9s41
77	174London(W.)173arr.	9 26	10 6	....	....	...	1156	1 20	1 50	2 15	...	...	4 20	...	5 41	6 36	....	8 20	...	1115	1120	...

s Saturdays only.

1924

27. The 1966 SCTS rail tour train, previously seen in picture no. 25, passes under Brewers Lane Bridge, on its way to Gosport. (J. Scrace)

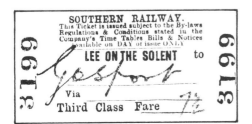

29. The Frater branch remained in use in 1986 to the Bedenham Depot only. In October 1982, a RCTS railtour was curtailed at the Frater Gates, owing to the Falklands crisis. (D.J. Kemp)

28. No. 33112 waits for outgoing goods from the Bedenham (Frater) branch to be attached, on 7th February 1986. In the background is Tichborne Way bridge (formerly Admiralty Arch) from which the previous picture was taken. (D.J. Kemp)

30. The Admiralty sidings were opened in June 1911 and have been little photographed due to security restrictions. An MOD Hunslet runs south towards the main line. (W.L. Jenkins/Gosport Railway Society collection)

31. Another Admiralty line diverged south from the Frater branch to Priddy's Hard. RH766 is seen crossing Green Lane bound for the Hard. (D.J. Kemp)

32. Ministry of Defence staff, management and their invited guests gather to travel on the last train. The Bedenham line hit the local headlines after part of a 40-wagon ammunition train exploded on 14th July 1950, injuring 19 people and breaking countless windows in the area. (D.J. Kemp)

33. The last train from Priddy's Hard ran on 14th January 1986, leaving Bedenham and Elson as the only depots with rail connection to the Gosport branch. (D.J. Kemp)

34. Three miles from Fareham, the line ran through the only cutting on the branch and even that was shallow. It was spanned by Rowner Arch which was rebuilt not long before the RCTS special passed under, in March 1966. (S.C. Nash)

London South Western Ry.
STOKES BAY to
LEE ON THE SOLENT
Via Fort Brockhurst
Stokes Bay   Stokes Bay
Lee on Solent   Lee on Solent
THIRD   (S.1)   THIRD
CLASS   See over   CLASS
Fare 5½d   Fare 5½d

379

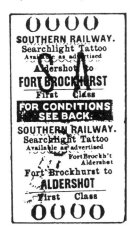

OOOO
SOUTHERN RAILWAY.
Searchlight Tattoo
Available as advertised
Aldershot to
FORT BROCKHURST
First Class
FOR CONDITIONS
SEE BACK
SOUTHERN RAILWAY.
Searchlight Tattoo
Available as advertised
Fort Brockh't
Aldershot
Fort Brockhurst to
ALDERSHOT
First Class
OOOO

36. An 1898 photograph reveals that improvements to the up side included provision of a canopy and glazing of the waiting area. The station name was just Brockhurst until May 1894. (Gosport Railway Society collection)

FORT BROCKHURST

35. The station was not built until about 25 years after the opening of the line by which time forts had been built at Rowner, Elson and Gomer also, to protect Portsmouth from a possible French attack from the west. The disc signal was rotated by a lever at the base of the post. The lamp is half way up the post. (NRM)

37. The Army made a substantial contribution to the station's income, particularly during the Boer War. There was a military prison nearby and the Garrison Church appears in this photograph of LSWR 2–4–0T no. 21 *Scott,* standing in the Lee-on-the-Solent bay platform, on 6th September 1899. (K. Nunn/LCGB)

The 1898 edition shows the Lee-on-the-Solent Railway passing through a gate after leaving the Gosport line. The 1875 siding and platform to the left of the level crossing initially served the Army; then it was used by RAF Grange and subsequently it was in Naval use, until 1964.

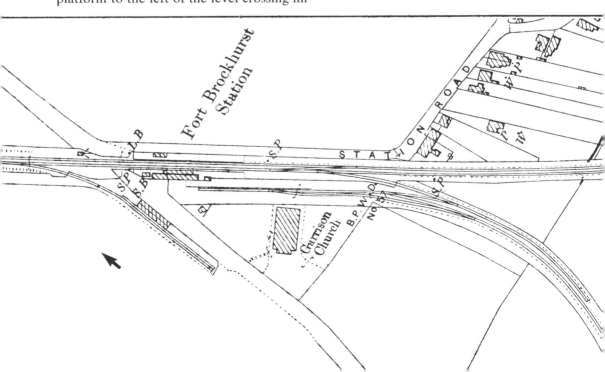

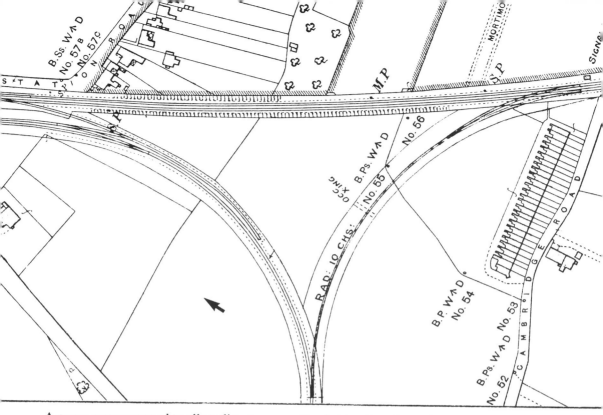

A curve was proposed to allow direct running from the branch to Gosport. This is shown, drawn onto the 1910 edition.

Cambridge Road crossing, on the right, was the scene of an exceptionally large number of accidents.

38. The second coach is one of a pair built for the Lee-on-the-Solent Railway by Brown Marshall & Co. of Birmingham in 1893, in time for the opening in 1894. The company never owned any locomotives, preferring to hire them from the LSWR.
(R.A. Emmerson/Pamlin Prints)

40. Steam was also to be found north of Fort Brockhurst station on occasions. "The Wheatsheaf" still stands at the junction of Brockhurst Road with Junction Road and the station house remains in use as a dwelling. (J.C. Lawrence/Gosport Railway Society collection)

39. This charming engine was the second to work on the line. She was built in 1862. Prior to being purchased by the LSWR in 1879 she was given the name "Lady Portsmouth". Examine her features in detail, particularly the distinctive fluted safety valve covers. The van behind her is a unique LSWR fruit van. (Lens of Sutton)

41. The decaying wayside station assumed unexpected importance when Her Majesty the Queen (before her Coronation) arrived on 21st November 1952, on her way to the Royal Naval Air Station at Lee-on-the-Solent. Mayor Osborn is greeting her, on the down platform. (J.C. Lawrence/Gosport Railway Society collection)

42. A class 700, wheezing from her inside cylinders, plods away from Fort Brockhurst on 30th May 1953 with a mixture of wagons, so typical of the post-war years. (L. Elsey)

44. A child in arms is encouraged to witness the departure of class M7 0–4–4T no. 30479 northwards. No wonder most boys wished to become engine drivers. (D. Cullum)

0580

SOUTHERN RAILWAY.
Issued subject to the Bye-laws, Regulations & Conditions in the Company's Bills and Notices.
H.M.F. or LEAVE.
Fareham to
FORT BROCKHURST
Third Class
NOT TRANSFERABLE
SOUTHERN RAILWAY.
H.M.F. or LEAVE
Fort Brockhurst
Fareham
Fort Brockhurst to
FAREHAM
Third Class
0580

0193

SOUTHERN RLY.
DAY EXCURSION
Available as advertised
WATERLOO to
FORT BROCKHURST
Third Class
FOR CONDITIONS SEE BACK
SOUTHERN RLY.
DAY EXCURSION
Available as advertised
F. B'khurst
Waterloo
Fort Brockhurst to
WATERLOO
Third Class
0193

43. The young train spotter appears to have parked his pedal car in the waiting shelter whilst his mother and the driver of the Ford van are forced to gaze at class L11 no. 30412 as it runs in with two coaches for Gosport. (D. Cullum)

45. The signal arm appears to be the early LSWR tapered wooden pattern but the spectacles are unusual. The hut is thought to pre-date the signal box and may have been for the benefit of the crossing keeper. (D. Cullum)

46. A down freight creeps through behind class Q1 no. 33025. Over the years, the station house had acquired an assortment of chimney pots and the end wall had been slated to prevent damp penetration. (Lens of Sutton)

47. The lattice signal post was replaced by one made from two running rails; the platform canopy was removed but the garden shed style signal box remained in use. In 1933, the Traffic Manager requested that the Chief Engineer raise the line speed limit from 30 to 45 mph so that the loop at Fort Brockhurst could be abolished. Having obtained the speed increase, the loop was then retained. (A.F.E. Field)

48. Q class no. 30543 proceeds down the short remaining portion of the Lee-on-the-Solent branch on 21st October 1955, in order to shunt coal wagons into the former bay line. Photograph no. 58 in *Steaming through East Hants* (Middleton Press) shows an earlier part of this operation. Until about 1953, over ½ mile of the branch remained in use for coal traffic for C.H. House & Sons. (P. Hay)

49. The loop ceased to be used in November 1957, when a direct connection to the bay line was laid in and the signal box was reduced to the status of a ground frame. Class N 2–6–0 no. 31411 is seen hauling the SCTS *Southdown Venturer* on 20th February 1966. (J.H. Bird)

50. Many photographs were taken of the railtour on 20th March 1966 – this one has the merit of showing the new upper quadrant signal and the staff cabbage patch.
(D. Fereday Glenn)

SOUTHERN RAILWAY.
PRIVILEGE TICKET.
Issued subject to the conditions (a) on the Privilege Ticket Order and (b) on the back hereof.
Available for One day including day of issue
FORT BROCKHURST TO
MIDHURST
Via
FIRST CLASS

020 020

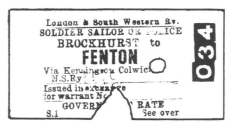

London & South Western Ry.
SOLDIER SAILOR OR POLICE
BROCKHURST to
FENTON
Via Kensington Colwick
M.S.Ry
Issued in exchange
for warrant No
GOVERN   RATE
S.1   See over

034 034

51. Steam traction in the Southern Region ceased in 1967 and so "The Hampshireman" on 3rd November 1968 was diesel hauled (no. 6506). An obsolete telephone pole serves as a reminder that this was the route of the first electric telegraph between Whitehall and the Dockyard. It was designed by Wheatstone and Cook and came into use on 1st April 1845. (J.H. Bird)

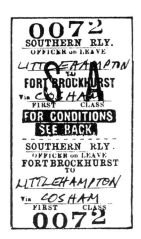

LEE-ON-THE-SOLENT BRANCH

52. There were three intermediate stopping points, the first being Fort Gomer Halt, a little over a mile down the branch. Until October 1909, it was called Privett but this was liable to cause confusion with the station of the same name on the Meon Valley Line. This is a 1961 view of the remains. (Gosport Railway Society collection)

53. Browndown Halt was nearly two miles from the junction and periodically had heavy miliary traffic from the nearby camp and ranges. (Lens of Sutton)

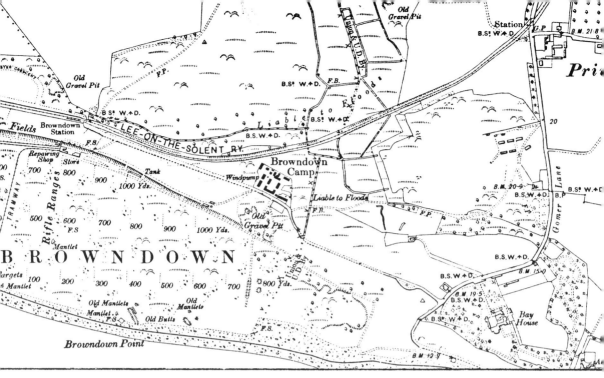

The 6" scale map of 1906 shows three narrow gauge lines on Browndown Ranges. These carried movable targets – the "Repairing Shop" was no doubt kept busy.

54. Elmore Halt was added on 11th April 1910 to serve the developing residential area. The other two halts were opened with the line and all three were closed on 1st May 1930, seven months ahead of the branch closure. (Gosport Railway Society collection)

LEE-ON-THE-SOLENT

55. Development of the area commenced in 1884 when Sir John Robinson planned a building scheme that was to rival Bournemouth. An essential feature of a worthwhile resort was a pier – this was opened 1888 – and the station (right of centre) followed within six years. (C. Hayward collection)

The 1910 map shows a crossover part way along the loop which allowed incoming wagons to be put on one end of the eastern part of the loop and outgoing ones to be removed from the other end.

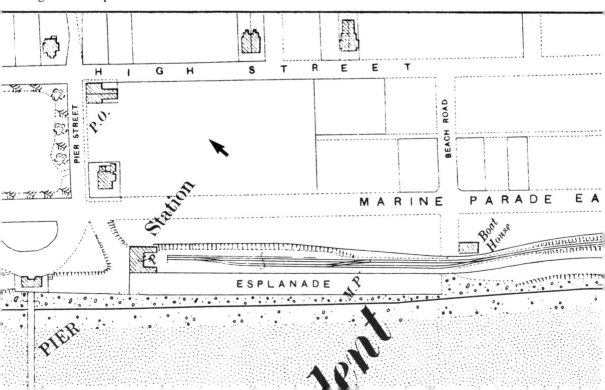

56. In addition to the two new bogie coaches, the company owned one second-hand four-wheeled four-compartment coach, with raised roof over the brake and luggage section. The locomotive is no. 392 in LSWR stock and was built by Manning Wardle. See also picture no. 39. (C. Hayward collection)

1924

FORT BROCKHURST and LEE-ON-THE-SOLENT.—Southern.

Miles		mrn	mrn	aft	aft	aft	aft	aft	aft	Miles		mrn	mrn	aft	aft	aft	aft	aft	aft
	Week Days only.										**Week Days only.**								
8	Fort Brockhurst dep.	9 10	1035	1235	2 45	4 5	4 48	6 15	7 15	8	Lee-on-the-Solent dep.	9 40	1125	1 10	3 40	4 25	5 15	6 55	7 55
—	Fort Gomer Halt	9 13	1038	1238	2 48	4 8	4 51	6 18	7 18	—	Elmore Halt..........	9 43	1128	1 13	3 43	4 28	5 18	6 58	7 58
—	Browndown Halt.....	9 18	1043	1243	2 53	4 13	4 56	6 23	7 23	—	Browndown Halt	9 47	1132	1 17	3 47	4 32	5 22	7 2	8 2
—	Elmore Halt..........	9 22	1047	1247	2 57	4 17	5 0	6 27	7 27	—	Fort Gomer Halt [171	9 51	1136	1 21	3 51	4 36	5 26	7 6	8 6
3	Lee-on-the-Solent arr.	9 26	1051	1251	3 1	4 21	5 4	6 31	7 31	3	Fort Brockhurst . arr.	9 56	1141	1 26	3 56	4 41	5 31	7 11	8 11

57. A postcard view from the pier shows the spacious station building and a locomotive running round its train. Fishing was about the only industry at Lee and may have provided some rail traffic. (Lens of Sutton)

58. One of the locomotives used by the LSWR on the branch was no. 734, an ex-LBSCR Terrier 0–6–0T. It had been acquired for use on the Lyme Regis branch and subsequently had a long and varied career which is outlined in our *Branch Line to Hayling*, under its original number (46). It now operates on the Isle of Wight Steam Railway and was photographed here in about 1912. (Lens of Sutton)

59. The flat bottom rails of the previous picture were replaced by bullhead ones, seen here. Two additional sidings were laid temporarily on the sea side of the loop in 1918, to receive materials for the construction of a seaplane station. Here we see Terrier no. B661 on 14th February 1928. (H.C. Casserley)

60. Features of note here are the wagons attached to the coaches; the locomotive water filler beyond the whistle board and the ex-LSWR coaches with centre vestibules. The coaches were fitted for push-pull working and had iron trellis gates at the vestibules. (A. Triggs collection)

61. The last passenger train was hauled by ex-LBSCR class D1 no. B626, on the last day of 1930. To the right of the seated railway officer is Mr. F.J. Marlow, station master and everything else. (M.F. Marlow/Gosport Railway Society)

62. The former station building is in use today as the Olympia Amusement Arcade, the decorative eaves on the north east elevation still being visible. The track was lifted in December 1935 to just beyond Elmore Halt and a further 1½ miles was removed in 1940. (Gosport Railway Society collection)

63. Another class D1 hauled the final goods train, which left on 29th October 1935. The company had remained independent until 1923 and in its heyday had a staff of eleven. (Gosport Museum collection.)

The Last Goods Train
From Lee-on-the-Solent
Oct: 2. 1935.

Forton

Brick Field

Cemetery

Kilns

Brick Field

Brick Field

Kiln

GOSPORT

Old Clay Pit

Old Clay Pit

Railway Station

The Grove

OKE and GOSPOR

Brick Field

Signal Post

B.M. 20

STOKES BAY BRANCH

Water Works

Bury Ho.

Bury Place

Stoke Ho.

Gosport Gas Works

Bury Farm

Bury Lodge

Bury

The White Hart Tavern

Jacobs Ladder

Dock Village Lane

Dock Village

Bury Hall

Green Lane

Stoke Road

King's Bastion

High Water Mark of Ordinary Tide

Alverstoke House of Industry (Parish Workhouse)

Victoria Place

EWER COMMON

Mud

Alverstoke Nat.l School (Boys)

Mount Pleasant

Heath Cottage

Gun Boat Yard

Burial Ground

St. Mary's Ch.

The Rectory

Little Anglesey

Old Gravel Pit

Alverstoke

Stoke Lake

Ford

High Water Mark of Ordinary

Cliff

Anglesey Lodge

Anglesey Crescent

Anglesey

St. Mark's Church (Chapel of Ease)

Signal Post

Haslar Hospital Cemetery

Claxhall Lane

Palestine Place

The Fighting Cocks (P.H.)

Claxhall

Chap. Cemetery

1870   6" scale

Coast Guard Station

Monckton House (Flagstaff)

Encamping Fields

Stokes Bay Pier

Terminus

Ford Lane

1921   6" scale

64. The branch diverged a little to the east of Lees Lane crossing, at what was earlier known as Forton junction. To the west, Cambridge Road crossing was provided with a resident keeper. (P. Keat collection)

65. A trailing siding from the down line was situated adjacent to Lees Lane Junction to serve the Ashley Wallpaper Works. It was laid in 1932 and received new machinery for the works direct from Germany, via the train ferry. (Gosport Railway Society collection)

66. The signal box ceased to be a block post when the line was singled in 1934 but remained in use until February 1968. The train passing the high-level clothes lines is the LCGB railtour on 3rd November 1968. (J.H. Bird)

The 1910 edition shows a ballast siding laid in 1901 for Mr. Relf, the contractor for the construction of the Meon Valley line.

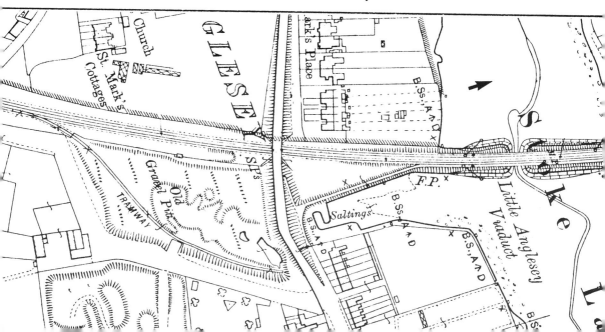

GOSPORT ROAD

67. Initially all trains for Stokes Bay ran into Gosport and reversed. After the western side of the triangular junction was completed, two trains a day started to run direct onto the branch (from 1st June 1864). A simple platform was provided, for the benefit of Gosport passengers, and was known as Stoke Road until November 1866. This northward view is from 1933. (Lens of Sutton)

68. This is the eastern side of the station viewed from Cleveland Road. The 1885 map named the footbridge "Jacobs Ladder", although the one seen here was erected in 1889. Station buildings and a carriage drive were provided on the opposite side in 1886. (Gosport Railway Society)

69. The platforms were lengthened in 1889 and canopies erected in 1896. This is the up platform, looking south in the early 1920s. (A. Triggs collection)

70. The up line was lifted in 1924 but the down track was retained for stock stabling, as seen here, until 1934. Note the centre birdcage look-out.
(Gosport Railway Society collection)

1898

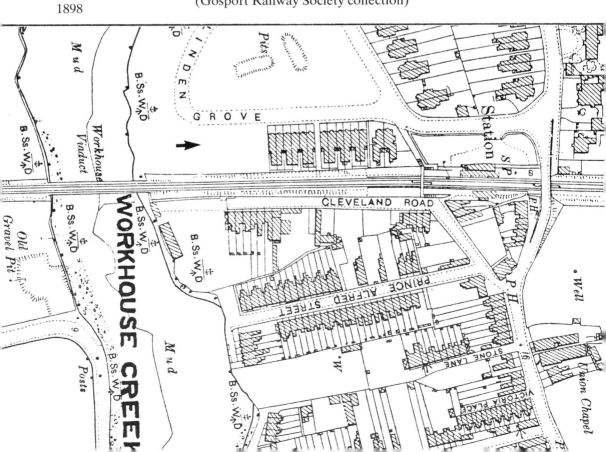

71. The crossing keeper's cottage in Crescent Road serves as a dwelling and is evidence of this long forgotten part of local history. (Gosport Railway Society collection)

2 MR 95

London & South Western Ry.
GOSPORT ROAD to
WATERLOO
Gosport Road   Gosport Road
Waterloo   Waterloo
THIRD   (S.3)   THIRD
CLASS   See over   CLASS
Fare 6/2   Fare 6/2

0523

SOUTHERN RAILWAY
This Ticket is issued subject to the By- and
Regulations & Conditions stated in the
Company's Time Table Bills & Notices
FORT BROCKHURST to
OXFORD
Via Basingstoke & G. W. Ry.
F. Brockhurst   F. Brockhurst
Oxford   Oxford
3rd CLASS   3rd CLASS
Fare 9/9   Fare 9/9

0523

STOKES BAY

72. The LSWR took full control of the line in 1875 and instituted a 2¾ hour service from Waterloo to Ryde. This was ½ hour quicker than travelling via Portsmouth but the advantage was lost the following year when Portsmouth Harbour station was opened. HMS *Iris* is on the right of this early view of the pier. (P. Keat collection)

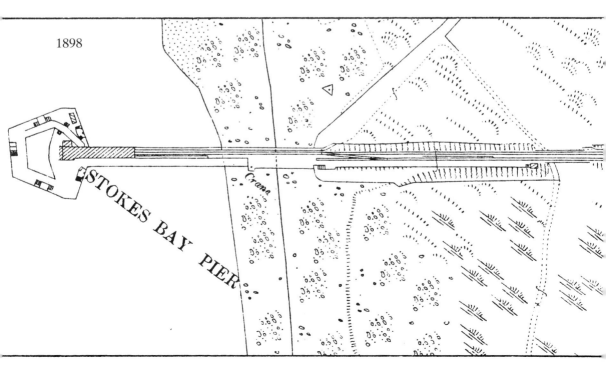

1898

STOKES BAY PIER

Crane

JOINT RAILWAY, SOUTHAMPTON, AND COWES COMPANIES' STEAM PACKET SERVICE

TO AND FROM THE

ISLE OF WIGHT

FROM JUNE 1st, 1901, UNTIL FURTHER NOTICE (weather &c., permitting)

S.S.

"Duchess of Fife"

"Alexandra"

"Duchess of Kent"

"Princess Margaret"

S.S.

"Duchess of Connaught"

"Duchess of Edinburgh"

"Duchess of Albany"

PORTSMOUTH TO RYDE.   Week Days.

	MAIL		S										S						S			T
S. HARBOUR dep	2.40	7.20	8.15		9.45	11.20		12.20	1.20	1.50		2.30	2.55	3.25	4.0		4.45		5.55	6.55		7.20	8.0	11.15
THSEA PIER ,,			8.30	9.45		11.30	12.25		1.30		2.35			3.35		4.50		5.45			7.0		8.10	
E PIER arr	3.10	7.50	8.45	8.55	10.10	10.15	11.55	12.50	12.50	1.55	2.20	3.0	3.0	3.25	4.0	4.30	5.15	5.15	6.10	6.25	7.25	7.50	8.35	11.45

RYDE TO PORTSMOUTH.   Week Days.

			S				S						S					S			MAIL	T
E PIER dep	7.15	8.5	8.55	10.10	10.15	11.15	12.20	1.0		1.5	2.0	2.30	3.0	3.55	4.0	5.0	5.20	5.40	6.15	6.30	7.20	7.55	8.45	9.20	11.50
THSEA PIER arr		8.30			10.40	11.40	12.45	1.25				2.55	3.25	4.20			5.45	6.5		6.55		8.20	9.10	
TS. HARBOUR arr	7.45	8.35	9.25	10.40		11.50	12.55		1.35	2.30	3.0	3.35			4.30	5.30			6.45		7.50			9.55	12.20

Portsmouth to Ryde.   SUNDAYS.

T Thursdays only

	MAIL		S					S						S		
TS. HARBOUR dep	2.40		8.45	10.0	11.45	12.15		2.20		3.0			5.40	6.45	7.20		8.5
THSEA PIER			8.45		10.10		12.25		2.40	3.10	4.10	5.45		6.55		8.10	
E PIER arr	3.10	9.10	9.15	10.35	12.15	12.45	12.50	2.50	3.5	3.35	4.35	6.10	6.10	7.20	7.50	8.35	8.35

NOTE.—Boats marked S are th Southampton and Cowes Steam Packe Companies' Boats, tickets betwee Southsea Pier and Ryde being no available by either the Joint Railwa Companies' Steam Boats or the South ampton and Cowes Steam Boats betwe Ryde and Southsea Pier.

Ryde to Portsmouth.   Sundays.

			S		S				S				S		S	MAIL
E PIER dep	7.50	9.20	10.35	11.0	12.20	1.0	1.0	3.5	4.35	5.5	5.5	6.15	7.35	7.35	8.10	8.40	9.20
THSEA PIER arr		9.45	11.0	11.25	12.45	1.25		3.30	5.0		5.30	6.40	8.0		8.35	9.0	
TSMOUTH HARBOUR arr	8.20	9.55		11.35	12.55		1.30			5.35	5.40	6.50		8.5			9.55

STOKES BAY TO RYDE.   Week Days. | RYDE TO STOKES BAY.

STOKES BAY dep	8.47	9.30	10.45	11.40	2.40	5.5	6.50		RYDE PIER dep	9.8	10.10	11.15	2.0	4.0	6.15
RYDE PIER arr	9.7	9.50	11.5	12.0	3.0	5.25	7.10		STOKES BAY arr	9.28	10.30	11.35	2.20	4.20	6.35

Fares :—To Ryde Pier Head and vice versa

From	Single 1st	Single 2nd	Return 1st	Return 2nd	
Portsmouth Har. Southsea Pier	1/1	9d.	1/8	1/2	Including Ports. Har. or Southsea but Exclusive of Ryde Pier Tolls
Stokes Bay.	1/-	8d.	1/6	1/-	Exclusive of Pier Tolls

Fares :—To Ryde Pier Gates and vice versa

From	Single 1st	Single 2nd	Return 1st	Return 2nd	
Portsmouth Har. Southsea Pier	1/3	11d.	2/-	1/6	Including Pier Tolls but Exclusive of Tramway and Train.
Stokes Bay.	1/2	10d.	1/10	1/4	

RETURN TICKETS ARE AVAILABLE EITHER ROUTE AND FOR TWO DAYS (including day of issue and return).

Those issued on Saturday are available to return on the following Monday. Children between three and twelve are charged half-fares.

The connection between the Trains and Boats and vice versa is not guaranteed, neither will the Joint Companies be accountable for any loss, inconvenience, or injury arising from sea risks or delays.

Passengers are requested to look to their luggage on entering and leaving the Steam Packets, and before embarking to see it labelled to the Station or Pier where the journey of the owner terminates.   First Class passengers allowed 120lbs., Second Class 100lbs., Third Class 60lbs.   Excess will be charged according to tariff.

Goods or Merchandise not allowed as passengers' luggage, and will be charged for at Parcels Tariff.

SEASON TICKET RATES.—First Class, Twelve Months, £6. Six Months, £3 10s. Three Months, £2.   Available for all advertised passages between Stokes Bay Ryde, and the Piers at Portsmouth, including Pier Toll at Southsea Pier and Portsmouth Harbour Station. Children under 15 years of age half these rates.

Season Tickets are issued to Scholars up to 18 years of age, including Pier Toll at Southsea Pier and Portsmouth Harbour Station. Twelve Months, £3. Six Months. £1 15s. Three Months, £1.

Quarterly Tickets may be extended to six or twelve months on payment of the difference between the periodical rates, but tickets must be promptly renewed or the privilege will be forfeited For each ticket a deposit of 5s. is required.   It will be refunded on return of the ticket (which is the property of the Joint Companies) not later than the day of expiry.

TOW BOATS for conveyance of Horses, Carriages, Live Stock and Merchandise between Portsmouth and Ryde, leave Portsmouth for Ryde, week days (weather permitting) about 8.45 a.m. and 1 p.m., and Ryde for Portsmouth about 10 a.m. and 3 p.m.

Senders or Owners of Goods, Horses, Carriages, Live Stock, &c., by Tow Boats, take upon themselves all risk of conveyance, and of loading or unloading, as the Companies will not be answerable for accidents or damage done to any Property, Live Stock, &c. All Goods, Cattle, &c., must be in the place of embarkation half-an-hour before the time of sailing, and in charge of Senders' or Owners' Servants, who must accompany them.

Drovers in charge of not less than 3 Beasts, 10 Sheep or Pigs, in Tow Boat free, but must pay ordinary fares returning.   All charges to be prepaid if required.

Offices :—Portsmouth Town Station ; Portsmouth Harbour Station ; Point, Portsmouth ; Esplanade Station, Ryde.

BY ORDER

31.

W. H. BARRELL, PRINTER, 114 HIGH STREET PORTSMOUTH.

73. The pier required extensive repairs in 1896, which cost £6,000. The route remained at a disadvantage to the more direct one until closure on 1st November 1915.
(Gosport Railway Society collection)

STOKES BAY
S.1   TO
RYDE PIER
Exclusive of Tramway
and Train
1st Class
Fare 1/10
3054

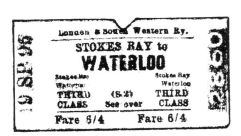

London & South Western Ry.
STOKES BAY to
WATERLOO
Stokes Bay   Stokes Bay
Waterloo   Waterloo
THIRD   (S.2)   THIRD
CLASS   See over   CLASS
Fare 6/4   Fare 6/4

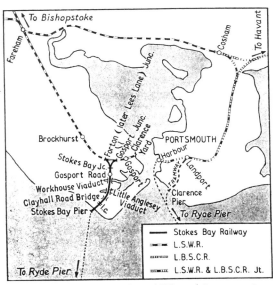

The Stokes Bay Railway, about 1876, and its connections with the L.S.W.R. and L.B.S.C.R.

(Railway Magazine)

74. In its last years it was only used in the summer, as south-westerly gales could prevent the ferry boats reaching the pier safely. The pier and track northwards (almost to Gosport Road station) were purchased by the Admiralty in 1922 and the rails were lifted (except on the pier) in the 1930s. This 1955 view shows one of the two cranes added by the Navy. (Gosport Museum collection)

London and South Western Ry.

787

FROM WATERLOO TO

STOKES BAY

---

75. The station master was a much respected member of the staff and of the community. A record of the object to which this plaque was attached has not survived.
(Gosport Railway Society collection)

PRESENTED TO MR. J.C.GARNHAM. by the Staffs of GOSPORT, GOSPORT ROAD & STOKES BAY STATIONS UPON HIS RETIREMENT from the L & S W R COMPANY'S SERVICE. DEC. 31ST 1911

GOSPORT

76. An engraving, dated 21st December 1841, shows one of the impractical features of the design. The pillar of the archway to the right of the locomotive was dangerously close to the track and was later removed. Several carriage doors were damaged on it and maybe passengers heads also. (N.R.M.)

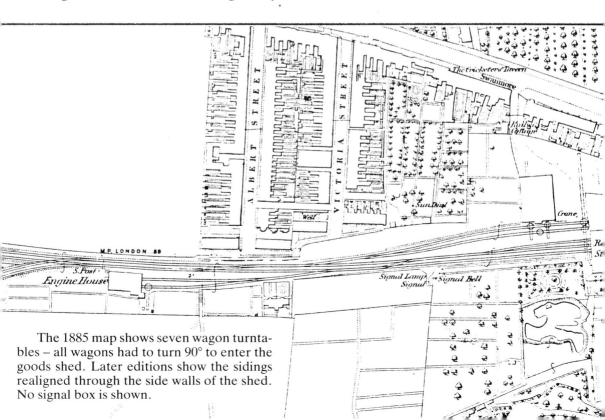

The 1885 map shows seven wagon turntables – all wagons had to turn 90° to enter the goods shed. Later editions show the sidings realigned through the side walls of the shed. No signal box is shown.

77. The terminus was inconveniently situated over ½ mile from the Portsmouth ferry berth. The street tramway, in the foreground, made the transfer easier after it was opened in 1882. The vessel right of centre is the "floating bridge", a service that was maintained until 1959. A closer view is to be found in our *Portsmouth to Southampton* album. (Hampshire County Library)

Ferry fares :—½d. each person ; cycles, 1d. each ; fares for carriages or motors (by floating bridge): Single, 9d. ; return, 1/2.

The steam-launches and floating bridge start from Gosport Hard at intervals of six minutes, the former landing passengers close to Portsmouth Harbour Station, whence Park Road leads direct to the Town Hall, and the latter at " the Point," Old Portsmouth.

Steamers from the Isle of Wight land passengers at Stokes Bay Pier, whence Gosport Road Station is reached by a short railway journey through Anglesey, and across the Stoke and Workhouse Lakes, the main portion of Alverstoke being passed on the left. It should be borne in mind that Gosport Road Station (which is close to the Bury and Stoke Roads) is only half-a-mile from Alverstoke village.

A splendid service of electric-cars links up Gosport Hard with Forton, Ann's Hill, Brockhurst and Fareham ; and another excellent service connects the Hard with Bury Cross *via* Stoke Road, thus making Alverstoke, the Park, and Lee-on-the-Solent easily accessible.

First cars leave the Hard for Brockhurst and Fareham at 8.0, 8.15, and 8.30 a.m., and run every fifteen minutes afterwards until 11.15 p.m.

After 9.30 a.m. intermediate cars will be run between the Hard and Brockhurst (Elson Road) only, giving a seven-and-a-half minutes' service on this section until 10.15 p.m. On Sundays cars run every fifteen minutes between Gosport and Fareham after 1.30 p.m. A seven-and-a-half minutes' service will shortly be started on this section until 10.45 p.m. The first car from the Hard to Bury Cross starts at 8 a.m. on week-days, and there is a ten minutes' service until 10.45 p.m. Sundays, first car at 1.35 p.m., and a ten minutes' service until 10.15 p.m.

1910

78. The chimneys at each end of the station have been described as fenestrated or coupled. Either way they make a distinctive feature, more impressive than those at Fareham. The posters announce the Cherbourg service and trains on the new Southsea branch.

(Gosport Railway Society collection)

1898

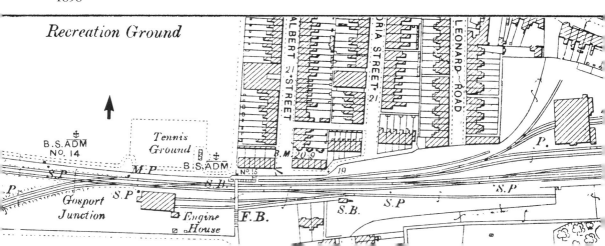

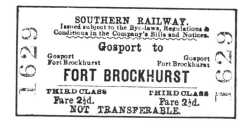

SOUTHERN RAILWAY.
Issued subject to the Bye-laws, Regulations &
Conditions in the Company's Bills and Notices.

Gosport to

Gosport   Gosport
Fort Brockhurst   Fort Brockhurst

FORT BROCKHURST

THIRD CLASS   THIRD CLASS
Fare 2½d.   Fare 2½d.
NOT TRANSFERABLE.

629

Gosport is traditionally supposed to have acquired its name from an event of the twelfth century, when, in the stress of a storm, Henry de Blois landed here on his return from Normandy.

So seemingly miraculous was the escape, that the famous Bishop of Winchester, brother of King Stephen, granted the inhabitants a charter, and decreed that the place should be called "God's Port." This was in 1158. For many years afterwards it was little more than a fishing village, sharing, with Portsmouth, attacks from the French—there being no "*entente cordiale*" in those days.

79. The left hand platform has mainly been used for goods, within living memory. No doubt the architect, William Tite, intended the platforms to be used for arrivals and departures. The ground signals and enamelled signs of the period add interest.
(Lens of Sutton)

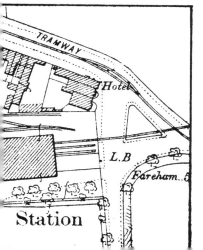

80. A 1906 view inside the colonnade shows the position of the booking office entrance to be close to the man on the right.
(Gosport Railway Society collection)

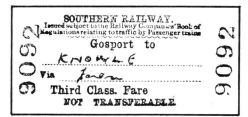

82. The station was the scene of many ceremonial occasions over the years. This example is the arrival of the Duke of Wellington's Regiment in 1924. Chaplin & Co, whose van stands in the background, were the local parcel cartage agent.
(Mrs. E. Hinton collection)

81. An Edwardian photograph records a group of craftsmen and labourers who were presumably carrying out repair work at the station. (Gosport Railway Society collection)

83. The driver leans out in an attempt to see a green flag whilst a boy looks up a trumpet to see how it works as the same regiment leaves in 1937, for new barracks in Plymouth. (Gosport Railway Society collection)

84. The elegant chimney stacks received assorted pots over the years without any aesthetic consideration. Likewise, additional offices were erected on the passenger platform. (Gosport Railway Society collection)

85. Gosport Junction can be seen beyond the locomotive as class A12 no. 644 comes off the single line with a down freight. Another locomotive stands on the former down line, which had been retained as a siding as far as the Ashley Wallpaper Works near Lees Lane Junction.
(Lens of Sutton)

86. Goods engines were sometimes used on local passenger trains in the summer when no train heating was required. This example is no. 350, an 0–6–0 of class 700, and is seen on 31st May 1937. The iron support for the brickwork replaced the arch seen in the early engraving. (NRM)

0050
SOUTHERN RLY
PRIVILEGE TICKET
Available for One Month
including day of issue & return
Issued subject to the Con-
ditions (a) on the Privilege
Ticket Order and (b) on the
back hereof
LEE ON THE SOLENT
to FORT BROCKHURST
Third Class
SOUTHERN RAILWAY
PRIVILEGE TICKET
Available for ONE Week
including DAY of Issue
Fort Brockhurst
Lee on Sol't
Fort Brockhurst to
LEE ON THE SOLENT
Third Class
0050

Lee-on-the-Solent-Ry
LEE ON THE SOLENT
S.1   TO
FORT BROCKHURST
2nd Class
Fare 1/-
063

87. Tite employed the idea of external stone arches with recessed arched windows at Southampton Terminus but the result was insignificant without the massive fifteen col- umns erected here. He would not have approved of the extra chimney stack or the iron arch support. (Lens of Sutton)

88. Another 1937 view shows the columns of the colonnade to have rather small and plain capitals. Behind the facade, an interesting experiment took place that year with a petrol driven Michelin railcar, fitted with rubber wheels but steel flanges. It was only eight feet high! (NRM)

89. St. Vincent Boy Cadets leaving for their war-time base, a holiday camp on the Isle of Man, in September 1939. (J.C. Lawrence)

90. Seldom was the goods platform not obscured by vans and wagons. This photograph must date from the early days of World War II as the platform edge had been whitened and the pillar painted with black and white bands to aid personal navigation in the "black out". (Lens of Sutton)

91. The engine release crossover and the through line to Clarence Yard are seen in this last view of the massive timber roof trusses. They were totally destroyed during an air raid on 10th March 1941. Goods Porter Gates was commended for summoning the crew of a locomotive from an air raid shelter to draw out the wagons from under the blazing roof. (Lens of Sutton)

92. The locomotive shed was also destroyed by a bomb of an evil type – it remained unexploded in the ground for 24 hours. This single road shed was erected in its place. Prior to WWI, there were six pairs of locomotive crews and three shed staff on duty here.
(Gosport Railway Society collection)

94. U class no. 31805 stands at the head of the 12.45 to Eastleigh on a grey day in early December 1952, when passenger traffic was very much in decline. (S.C. Nash)

93. The station never recovered its dignity, remaining more like a Grecian relic of great antiquity ever since. Who would believe this to be an operational passenger terminus? (H.C. Casserley)

95. The class M7 0-4–4Ts were economical locomotives for lightly loaded branch lines. The safety valve of no. 30053 is just "feather-ing". More seats arrived after the war and so did two lean-to buildings. (Gosport Railway Society collection)

97. A 4 mph speed limit was imposed on trains crossing the roads to Clarence Yard. This one is returning from the yard behind a class T9 and is passing over a green triangle at the road junctions, whilst cyclists wait in Mumby Road. (D. Cullum)

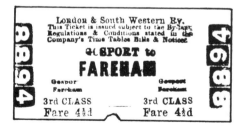

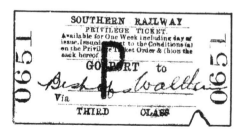

96. The heavy wooden roof trusses were replaced by lighter steel ones in 1947 but cladding was asbestos and was limited to the goods area with only a few sheets to protect passengers. Such were the effects of post-war economies on railway architecture. (A.F.E. Field)

98. The final configuration of the signalling is seen here. The ringed arm on the right was for shunting into the goods yard and the ground signal on the left controlled entry to the turning triangle. (D. Cullum)

→

100. The exterior was photographed on the same day to show the gates which swung across Spring Garden Lane when trains were crossing to Clarence Yard. Another set of gates protected Mumby Road. (J.H. Aston)

99. On 3rd May 1953, the Stephenson Locomotive Society ran a special train, seen here being shunted by another but cleaner M7. The photograph also reveals the location of Stokes Bay junction signal box, which eventually closed at the end of November 1957. (S.C. Nash)

101. The photograph of the last public passenger train on 6th June 1953 seems to have suffered from bad storage. The locomotive is Q class 0–6–0 no. 30546 ex-SR, whilst the van on the left is ex-LNER.
(Gosport Railway Society collection)

102. The gaps in the roof were an advantage on 28th March 1962 when U class no. 31808 was discharging smoke, whilst waiting for the level crossing gates to be opened.
(D. Fereday Glenn)

103. Class Q1 no. 33020 backs towards Clarence Yard in May 1962. The first of these locomotives were built during World War II and were known as "Austerities". The gas lamp adds a touch of antiquity to this study in light and shade. (D. Fereday Glenn)

104. The SCTS "Southdown Venturer" was described as the first passenger carrying train on the branch since 1953. The N class is photographed from every angle as it runs round its train on 20th February 1966. (D. Fereday Glenn)

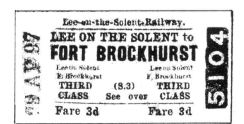

Lee-on-the-Solent Railway.
LEE ON THE SOLENT to
FORT BROCKHURST
Lee on Solent   Lee on Solent
to Brockhurst   to Brockhurst
THIRD   (8.3)   THIRD
CLASS   See over   CLASS
Fare 3d   Fare 3d

106. The next rail tour was organised by the LCGB only a month later. It started from Eastleigh at 12.15 and also traversed the Fawley and Lymington branches. A mobile crane on the left was provided for coal handling. (S.C. Nash)

105. Turning round on the footbridge a few minutes later, we witness the departure of the train with microphones protruding from the leading coach. The turning triangle and locomotive shed have gone – only the inspection pit remains as evidence of the latter. (J. Scrace)

London & South Western Ry.
This Ticket is issued subject to the Regulations
& Conditions stated in the Company's Time
Tables & Bills

(S.1) SOLDIER
FORT BROCKHURST to
BRIGHTON
Via Havant & L.B.& S.C.Ry

Issued in exchange
for warrant No.

3rd CLASS GOVERNMENT RATE

→

108. The deserted station reveals the two overhead gantries provided for transferring heavy loads from rail wagons to road vehicles. The 1938 handbook of stations quotes Gosport as having a 15-ton capacity crane. (J.H. Bird)

107. The footbridge from which many of the earlier pictures were taken now appears, as no. D6515 arrives with the morning freight on 9th September 1968. The photographer is close to the site of the signal box which in 1935 had 19 levers in use and 17 spare. (J.H. Bird)

→

109. The LCGB "Hampshireman" reaches its destination on 3rd November 1968, behind D6506. The goods platform retained its gas lights to the end. In 1963 the station had been designated "of special architectural interest" and in 1974 Hampshire County Council found itself responsible for the relic but little care has been taken of it. (J.H. Bird)

110. A few minutes later, the class 33 pushes the weeds aside, ready to run round its train. By then, all points were hand worked, their levers being the only items within sight to boast any paint. (J.H. Bird)

112. The goods loading bay on the right was added after WWII. A loading gantry can be seen projecting through the canopy valance. The former Station Hotel on the left was Pickford's Depository in 1969 and the building on the right was used as the passenger booking office, after the war. (Gosport Railway Society collection)

111. This CCT van appears in the previous three pictures, having become a static goods shed for the commercial department and is seen here in October 1969. Being unfit to move, it was abandoned, goods services having ceased in January of that year. (J.H. Bird)

113. To this day, the roof-less structure remains standing, awaiting a new use. The inner gates were not visible in picture no. 100, being obscured by larger gates in line with the kerb stones. (L. Campbell)

115. Queen Victoria acquired the Osborne Estate near East Cowes in 1845 and had a station constructed within the Yard to enable her journeys to the Isle of Wight to be undertaken in privacy. This drawing gives an impression of the structure in 1890. (Gosport Railway Society collection)

114. The Admiralty moved its victualling facilities from Portsmouth to Gosport in 1828 because of excessive thieving in that honourable city. The military and naval establishments were protected from invasion by a rampart, with a moat each side. Whilst the moats were partly filled, the railway had to pass through the other defence.
(A.E. Bennett)

117. A lantern slide records the end of the Queen's mainland journey. Her son became King Edward VII. He gave Osborne House away (to the nation), preferring "mainland fun". The line to the Yard then continued its routine task of transport of stores of every type. Meat, for example, was conveyed "on the hoof" to the Naval abbatoir. Coal was actually taken away from the Yard to supply Bedenham Depot.
(Gosport Railway Society collection)

116. A lavish waiting room was provided for Her Majesty, who used to travel to the Island twice a year in normal circumstances. It has been demolished but part of the train shed remains, walled up to form a store.
(Gosport Railway Society collection)

118. As at Portsmouth, the Admiralty refused to have the defences penetrated by a railway but the Queen's wishes overruled this. The line to her private station was opened in 1845 and Admiralty use of it followed. A short length of track and the tunnel through the rampart can be seen from Weevil Lane today. (R. Seymour)

THE ROYAL ROUTE

THIS RAILWAY CARRIED QUEEN VICTORIA FROM GOSPORT
STATION TO H.M. WAITING ROOM AND LANDING PLACE IN
THE ROYAL CLARENCE YARD ON HER FREQUENT JOURNEYS
BETWEEN LONDON AND OSBORNE, ISLE OF WIGHT AND FOR
FLEET REVIEWS.

GOSPORT STATION WAS BUILT IN CLASSICAL COLONNADE
STYLE IN 1842 BEFORE THE PORTSMOUTH LINE AND SAW
MANY ROYAL TRAINS PASS AND MANY STATE MESSAGES
WERE DISPATCHED BY WIRE.

ON HER DEATH IN 1901 THE QUEEN'S REMAINS LAY IN
H.M. WAITING ROOM IN ROYAL CLARENCE YARD BEFORE
FINALLY PASSING THIS WAY FOR LONDON.

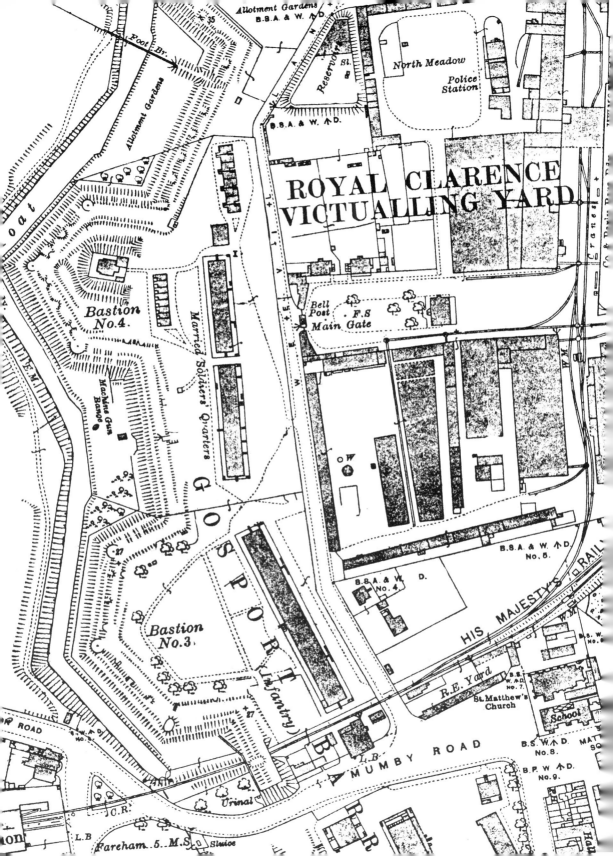

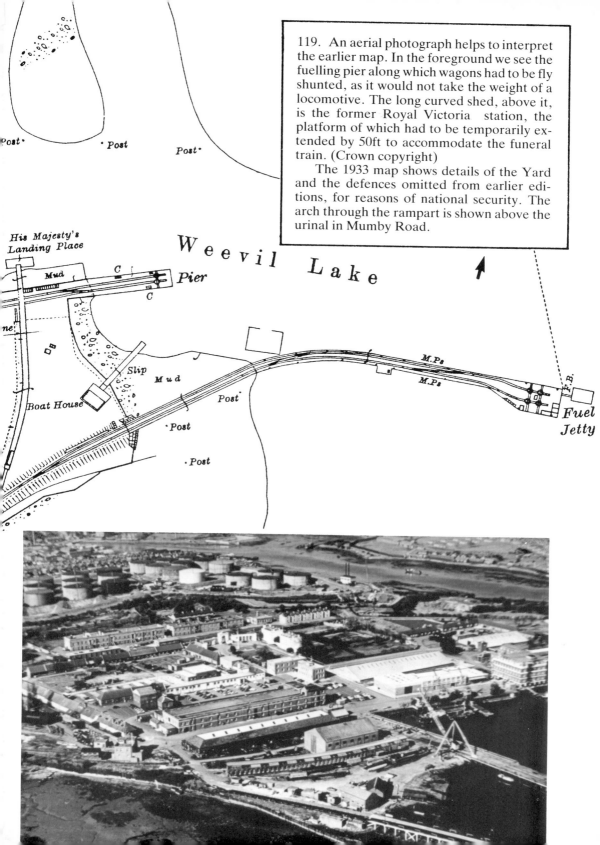

His Majesty's
Landing Place

W e e v i l   L a k e

Mud

C

Pier

C

ne

B

Slip

M u d

Boat House

Post

·Post

·Post

M.P.s

M.P.s

F.B.

Fuel
Jetty

119. An aerial photograph helps to interpret the earlier map. In the foreground we see the fuelling pier along which wagons had to be fly shunted, as it would not take the weight of a locomotive. The long curved shed, above it, is the former Royal Victoria station, the platform of which had to be temporarily extended by 50ft to accommodate the funeral train. (Crown copyright)

The 1933 map shows details of the Yard and the defences omitted from earlier editions, for reasons of national security. The arch through the rampart is shown above the urinal in Mumby Road.

Post·

· Post

Post·

LONDON AND SOUTH WESTERN RAILWAY
AND
LONDON BRIGHTON AND SOUTH COAST RAILWAY.

Station Masters and Heads of Departments must see that a copy of this Notice is handed to every person who may be in any way engaged in connection with the working of the Train, including Signalmen, Crossing Keepers, Flagmen and Fogmen, who must read it carefully, and strictly act up to and obey the instructions contained therein. No want of knowledge of these instructions can be accepted as an excuse for any failure or neglect of duty.

TO THE OFFICERS AND SERVANTS OF THIS AND OTHER COMPANIES CONCERNED.

FUNERAL TRAIN CONVEYING THE
BODY OF HER LATE MAJESTY QUEEN VICTORIA,
Accompanied by the Chief Mourner,
H.M. KING EDWARD VII.
AND
H.I.M. THE GERMAN EMPEROR
AND THE OTHER ROYAL PRINCES,

On SATURDAY, FEBRUARY 2nd, 1901.

FROM GOSPORT (S.W.R.) TO VICTORIA (*via Fareham, Cosham, Havant, Ford Junction, Horsham, Dorking and Mitcham Junction*):—
TIME TABLE.

UP JOURNEY.	PILOT. A.M. arr.	pass.	dep.	ROYAL TRAIN. A.M. arr.	pass.	dep.	UP JOURNEY.	PILOT. A.M. arr.	pass.	dep.	ROYAL TRAIN. A.M. arr.	pass.	dep.
Gosport (Clarence Yard, S.W.R.)	...	8 35		...	8 45		Stammerham Junction	...	9 52		10 2		
Gosport	8 38			8 48			Horsham	...	9 55		10 5		
Fareham	...	8 48	8 54	8 58			Warnham	...	9 58		10 8		
Cosham	8 57			9 7			Ockley	...	10 3		10 13		
Farlington Junction	9 0			9 10			Holmwood	...	10 6		10 16		
Havant Junction	9 5			9 15			Dorking	...	10 13		10 23		
Bosham	9 11			9 21			Leatherhead Junction ...	...	10 18		10 28		
Chichester	9 15			9 25			Epsom Junction	...	10 23		10 33		
Drayton	9 17			9 27			Sutton Junction	...	10 28		10 38		
Barnham Junction	9 22			9 32			Mitcham Junction	...	10 33		10 43		
Ford Junction	9 26			9 36			Streatham Junction South ...	...	10 37		10 47		
Arundel	9 30			9 40			Balham Junction (Main Line) ...	...	10 40		10 50		
Amberley	9 34			9 44			Clapham Junction	...	10 44		10 54		
Hardham Junction	9 39			9 49			Grosvenor Road (slowly) ...	...	10 48		10 58		
Pulborough	9 40			9 50			**Victoria**	...	10 50		11 0		
Billinghurst	9 46			9 56									

The Royal Train will consist of eight Vehicles.

On leaving Fareham, the Vehicles forming the Royal Train will run in the following order, viz.:— Brake Van, Saloon, Funeral Car, Royal Saloon, Saloon, Bogie First, Bogie First and Brake Van.

The Pilot Engine and the Engine of the Royal Train will carry the following Head Signals.

Clear Weather :—Three White Boards with a Double Diamond painted on them, one on top of Smoke Box and one on each end of Buffer Beam.

Foggy Weather :—Four Lights. A Green Light on top of Smoke Box, a Green Light on centre of Buffer Beam, and a White Light on each end of Buffer Beam.

120. The line gained fame on the occasion of Queen Victoria's funeral, although there was an embargo on photography. She died at Osborne House and her body was conveyed to Clarence Yard to commence the railway journey to Windsor via Victoria and Paddington. There was a procession through London whilst part of the train was transferred between the termini, via Addison Road (now Olympia). The LSWR provided class A12 no. 555 to take the Royal train to Fareham, from where it was hauled by LBSCR no. 54 *Empress*, illustrated here with funeral drapes. The sentiments influencing the choice of route are interesting. It is recounted that the Queen never again used Southampton after an occasion when the bill for the red carpet had been sent to Buckingham Palace. Many were surprised that the LBSCR route was chosen as the Queen had detested anything to do with Brighton, as that town had caused some unrecorded offence early in her reign. It is alleged that Portsmouth was also on the Queen's black list due to a display of anti-German feeling on one of her visits. It apparently took the form of a flagpole bearing a ladies undergarment together with a German sausage. Again, she was not amused.

MP Middleton Press

Easebourne Lane, Midhurst, West Sussex, GU29 9AZ
☎ Midhurst (073 081) 3169

BRANCH LINES
BRANCH LINES TO MIDHURST	0 906520 01 0
BRANCH LINES TO HORSHAM	0 906520 02 9
BRANCH LINE TO SELSEY	0 906520 04 5
BRANCH LINES TO EAST GRINSTEAD	0 906520 07 X
BRANCH LINES TO ALTON	0 906520 11 8
BRANCH LINE TO HAYLING	0 906520 12 6
BRANCH LINE TO SOUTHWOLD	0 906520 15 0
BRANCH LINE TO TENTERDEN	0 906520 21 5
BRANCH LINES TO NEWPORT	0 906520 26 6
BRANCH LINES TO TUNBRIDGE WELLS	0 906520 32 0
BRANCH LINE TO SWANAGE	0 906520 33 9

SOUTH COAST RAILWAYS
BRIGHTON TO WORTHING	0 906520 03 7
WORTHING TO CHICHESTER	0 906520 06 1
CHICHESTER TO PORTSMOUTH	0 906520 14 2
BRIGHTON TO EASTBOURNE	0 906520 16 9
RYDE TO VENTNOR	0 906520 19 3
EASTBOURNE TO HASTINGS	0 906520 27 4
PORTSMOUTH TO SOUTHAMPTON	0 906520 31 2

SOUTHERN MAIN LINES
WOKING TO PORTSMOUTH	0 906520 25 8
HAYWARDS HEATH TO SEAFORD	0 906520 28 2
EPSOM TO HORSHAM	0 906520 30 4
CRAWLEY TO LITTLEHAMPTON	0 906520 34 7

STEAMING THROUGH
STEAMING THROUGH KENT	0 906520 13 4
STEAMING THROUGH EAST HANTS	0 906520 18 5
STEAMING THROUGH EAST SUSSEX	0 906520 22 3

OTHER RAILWAY BOOKS
WAR ON THE LINE The official history of the SR in World War II	0 906520 10 X
GARRAWAY FATHER AND SON The story of two careers in steam	0 906520 20 7

OTHER BOOKS
MIDHURST TOWN – THEN & NOW	0 906520 05 3
EAST GRINSTEAD – THEN & NOW	0 906520 17 7
THE GREEN ROOF OF SUSSEX A refreshing amble along the South Downs Way	0 906520 08 8
THE MILITARY DEFENCE OF WEST SUSSEX	0 906520 23 1
WEST SUSSEX WATERWAYS	0 906520 24 X
BATTLE OVER PORTSMOUTH A City at war in 1940	0 906520 29 0